Dirt Bikes

Jesse Young

Reading consultant:

John Manning, Professor of Reading

University of Minnesota

CAPSTONE BOOKS

an imprint of Capstone Press
Mankato, Minnesota

Capstone Books are published by Capstone Press
151 Good Counsel Drive, P.O. Box 669, Mankato, Minnesota 56002
http://www.capstone-press.com

Library of Congress Cataloging-in-Publication Data
Young, Jesse, 1941–
    Dirt bikes/by Jesse Young.
    p. cm.—(Motorcycles)
    Includes bibliographical references and index.
    ISBN 1-56065-226-8 (hardcover)
    1. Trail bikes—Juvenile literature. 2. Motorcycling—Juvenile literature.
[1. Trail bikes. 2. Motorcycling.] I. Title. II. Series.
TL441.Y68 1995
669.227'5—dc20   94-22827

Editorial Credits

John Coughlan, editorial director; John Martin, managing editor;
    Gil Chandler, copy editor

Acknowledgments: A special thanks to Dan Cunningham, and SJ Eldred,
    Teen Reporter.

Table of Contents

Chapter 1

To the Trails

It's six o'clock in the morning, and you want to be out by eight for a full day of riding. You gather up your boots, gloves, goggles, and shoulder pads. You collect gasoline, extra brake and clutch levers, and a spare drive chain. You put a big lunch in your tool box.

You load the bike into the bed of the pickup truck, where tight straps hold it in place. You stack your gear next to the bike. At the last minute, you remember to bring your helmet.

After a long drive, you finally reach the trail. The countryside is perfect, with steep hills and twisting, turning paths. Riding your dirt bike here will be worth the trip.

Finally, you've reached the start of the trail. You quickly unload the bike and you suit up. With a kick, the bike roars to life. Ahead lies the thrill of the open trail–and of modern dirt-bike riding.

Chapter 2

Dirt Bikes for Work and Play

There are two basic types of motorcycles. One type is made for riding on smooth surfaces like roads or paved race tracks. These motorcycles are called road bikes. They are heavier, faster, and more powerful than off-road bikes.

Off-road motorcycles, or dirt bikes, are lighter than road bikes. Dirt bikes are built to handle rough **terrain** like dirt, mud and rocks.

Dirt Bikes for Work

Not all people use dirt bikes for sport. Some people need their dirt bikes for work. Members of the Royal Canadian Mounted Police ride Honda, Kawasaki, and Suzuki dirt bikes instead of horses. Forest rangers take dirt bikes out on patrol. Some cowboys even herd cattle from the seats of their dirt bikes.

Workers travel on dirt bikes deep into the woods to repair telephone equipment. Trappers, miners, and lumberjacks also use dirt bikes. The land they work on is often too rugged for anything else.

Most people ride dirt bikes for fun. They enjoy being outdoors and finding new places to ride. They can follow an old trail or blaze a new one. Riders feel free on their dirt bikes.

Racing a Dirt Bike

Many people use dirt bikes to experience the excitement of competition. Different types of dirt-bike racing include **motocross**, **supercross**, **trials**, and **enduro**.

Some dirt-bike races cover long distances. The Paris-Dakar enduro race covers 6,371 miles (10,250 kilometers). But supercross races take place on oval or circular tracks in indoor stadiums. Trials is not a race at all. A trials event tests a rider's skill and balance in driving over **obstacles** like boulders, logs, and streams.

Motocross racers test their skill in racing around a short, hilly course.

Chapter 3

Basic Dirt Bike Features

All dirt bikes share some basic
features–**knobby tires**, lightweight frames,
long-travel suspension, and two- or four-
stroke engines placed high and out of the way.

"Knobbies"

Knobby tires ("knobbies") give the dirt bike
good **traction** through mud, loose gravel, and
sand. Without knobby tires, you wouldn't have

**The knobbies on a dirt bike can handle the dirt and sand
on an open trail.**

much control on the rough trails. In deep sand you would find it difficult to move forward on regular tires. Although knobbies work well on natural surfaces, on a paved road they'll give you a bumpy ride.

The Suspension

Another important part of all dirt bikes is long-travel suspension. This includes the **fork legs** in the front and one or two **shock absorbers** in the rear. (Most modern dirt bikes have just one.) Long-travel suspension softens the ride over the big bumps.

The Engine

All dirt bikes have engines that are placed high in the **chassis** so they can clear obstacles such as large bumps, stumps, and rocks. The **exhaust pipe** also rides high so that it will not catch on boulders or fallen trees.

The engine rides high on the frame so obstacles in the trail won't damage it.

How It Works

Your dirt bike springs into action when a spark plug ignites a mixture of air and gasoline in the engine cylinder. The explosion moves a piston up and down inside the cylinder. This movement is called the **power stroke**.

A rod and a **crankshaft** convert the power stroke to a circular motion. This motion reaches the rear wheel by way of a clutch, a gearbox, and a drive chain.

Some dirt bikes have **two-stroke** engines. Others are **four-stroke**. In a two-stroke engine, there is a power stroke for every turn of the crankshaft. In a four-stroke, there is an extra stroke that lets out the exhaust. Every other turn of the crankshaft is a power stroke.

Every motorcycle, no matter how small, must have a way of cooling the hot-running engines. Air-cooled engines use metal fins to **dispel** the engine's heat. Water-cooled engines are more common today.

Chapter 4

Types of Dirt Bikes

Motocross Cycles

Motocross bikes must be light, but they must also be tough to handle the challenging tracks. Riders often have to deal with steep hills, tall jumps, and even trees.

A motocross cycle is usually used for racing. It has only the equipment necessary for riding off-road. It has no headlights and no taillights, no turn signals, no mirrors, no speedometer, and no kickstand.

All these bikes have small, two-stroke engines. Dirt-bike engines are measured in **cubic centimeters (cc)**. Common sizes for dirt-bike engines are 80cc, 125cc, 250cc and 500 cc. They are light but still give the motorcycle a lot of power.

The 16-inch (41-centimeter) wheels are held in place by telescopic-fork legs and a rear swing arm with one or two shock absorbers. The shock absorbers dampen the jolts. They soften landings after riding off large jumps during a race.

Dual-Purpose Bikes

Dual-purpose bikes have lights, turn signals, and speedometers. They are used on public streets as well as on off-road trails.

These bikes are best for the rider who likes to ride on the streets and on the trails but who does not want to buy two motorcycles.

For serious dirt-bike riders, dual-purpose bikes are too heavy. The dual-purpose bike does not make a very good street bike either.

Motocross tracks challenge riders with tough obstacles and rugged terrain.

The knobby tires and long-travel suspension make for a bumpy ride.

Enduro Bikes

The enduro bike is more rugged than the dual-purpose bike. It has head and taillights, a speedometer, and a **trip meter**. But unlike the dual-purpose bike, the enduro is not legal for the streets. Instead, it has become a popular racing bike.

The enduro race tests **endurance**. Competitors travel over rough trails for 50 to 150 miles (80 to 240 kilometers). According to the rules, they must keep a certain speed throughout the race. At checkpoints, judges make sure that the riders are not passing the speed limit. If you go too fast or too slow, you lose points. The rider who finishes closest to a set time is the winner.

An enduro rider leaps over a steep gorge with confidence.

Desert Riders

If you want to travel the deserts of North America or Africa, there is a sturdy dirt bike you can use. It is modeled after the bike used in the famous Paris-Dakar race from Paris, France to Dakar, Senegal. This event covers thousands of miles through the Sahara Desert, the hottest and driest place on earth.

The desert bike is fully legal, which means it has lights, turn signals, and mirrors. It also has a large fuel tank. Most of all, it is reliable. You wouldn't want your bike to break down in the middle of a desert.

Chapter 5

Choosing the Right Equipment

There are some things to think about when choosing your first dirt bike.

You should choose a bike that is not too tall. While seated, you should be able to touch both feet to the ground while slightly bending your legs.

Engine size is another consideration. Beginners often start with a dirt bike that has an engine of only 60 cubic centimeters (cc) (3.7 cubic inches). The largest ones are 600 cubic centimeters (36.6 cubic inches). Choose

a motorcycle with an engine size that matches your skill level. Too much power can be dangerous.

Get the Right Equipment

Good equipment is a must. The best riders in the world wear a full set of safety gear, and so should you. Always wear a helmet, goggles, jersey, pants, boots, gloves, and a chest protector.

• *Helmets* should fit snugly. Full-face helmets made of fiberglass offer the best protection.

• *Goggles* should also fit snugly to keep dust and dirt out of your eyes. Goggles with wide elastic straps and scratch-resistant lenses are best.

• *Jerseys* should be bright, so other riders can see you more easily.

• *Pants*–good-quality pants are made of a combination of nylon and leather and have inserts for plastic pads at the thighs and knees.

Good equipment is a must for all dirt-bike riders.

• *Boots* made of thick cowhide that cover the entire foot and shin are best.

• *Gloves* made of nylon with leather palms work best.

• *Chest protectors* provide some protection from flying dirt and rocks.

Chapter 6

Some Basic Skills

Dirt-bike riding is a tough sport that takes great skill. Every turn is a new challenge, but you'll get better every time you ride. If you do it the right way, dirt-bike riding can be fun.

The rules are simple. Don't try to do too much. And remember to concentrate. On the trail, you will face all kinds of dangers, from jagged stones to fallen trees. Handle your bike carefully. Ride only where allowed, and respect other people's property.

Hands and Feet Work Together

With a little practice, your hands and feet will begin to work together. The right hand controls the throttle and front brake. The left hand controls the clutch. The right foot is used for the rear brake pedal. The left foot shifts gears.

Hill Climbing

Here are some tips for climbing a hill:

1. Build up speed before the hill. If you don't have enough power at the bottom, you won't make it to the top.

2. Use the clutch and throttle properly. Keep the motor revved. If you use too much throttle, the rear wheel will spin and you'll lose traction.

3. For better control, balance your weight evenly on the bike. Stand up and stay loose. Move from side to side to keep your balance.

4. Follow a clear line to the top and stay with it. If your trail gets too difficult, **bulldog** it

to the top. If you still can't make it, slow down and let the bike fall to the side. Then turn around and go back down.

Downhill

Here are some tips for going downhill:

1. Once you have chosen your path, it is hard to go back. Stay on the path you've chosen. If you meet an obstacle, you can slow down, get off the bike, and walk it to easier terrain.

2. Use the clutch as well as the brakes to slow down. If you brake too hard, you'll start to skid.

3. Keep good body position. Stay balanced over the middle of the bike.

4. When you're going downhill, you often can't see where you're going. If you're not sure what's around a corner, bulldog it to the bottom.

5. If you're about to crash, save yourself before saving the bike.

Popping Wheelies

Wheelies can help you conquer obstacles. This is why popping a wheelie is one of the most important–and fun–skills to learn. Here's how to do it:

1. Make sure you are balanced on your bike and in control.

2. Use the clutch to get into the wheelie. With the clutch in, rev the engine. Then let the clutch out to "pop" the front wheel up.

3. Use the rear brake carefully so that you do not loop out. Tap the rear brake to keep from going back too far.

4. Don't be afraid to put out your knees for balance.

Chapter 7

Safety

These are some important points to remember when riding your dirt bike:

1. Always ride with someone. If you become seriously injured, you will not be able to help yourself if you're riding alone.

2. When in trouble, get off the bike. Don't hurry. Make it a rule with friends that you will always stop, wait, or help when someone is in trouble.

3. Don't try to do too much too soon. Don't try maneuvers that are beyond your skill level.

4. Always wear a helmet, riding pants, boots, goggles, and a chest protector. You'll feel more secure and you'll ride better.

5. Slow down when animals and people are around.

6. Never ride on private property unless given permission.

7. Use common sense.

Glossary

bulldog–to walk next to the bike with the engine running and the clutch engaged

chassis–the frame of a motorcycle

crankshaft–the main shaft of an engine. The pistons turn the crankshaft, which then turns the drive chain.

cubic centimeters (cc)–the size of the cylinder, or the area covered by the stroke of the piston

dispel–to get rid of something by scattering it

endurance–the ability to handle hardship or stress

enduro–a rugged racing bike made to run long distances

fork legs–metal tubes that hold the front wheel in place

exhaust pipe–pipe that allows waste gases to escape from the engine

four-stroke–a type of engine that uses an air intake and compression stroke as well as a power stroke

knobby tires–rugged tires with raised bumps that can handle sand, mud, and rough terrain

long-travel suspension–long, coiled springs and oil-filled dampers that cushion a bike against bumps

motocross–a race over dirt trails and natural terrain

obstacle–something that stands in the way of reaching a goal

power stroke–the stroke in a four-stroke engine in which the spark plug ignites the fuel mixture

shock absorbers–hydraulic devices that cushion the bumps of a rough surface

supercross–indoor motocross race

suspension–the system that cushions the motorcycle from hard bumps in the road or trail

terrain–the shape of the land

traction–the drawing or pulling of wheels along a road

trials–a competition that tests a rider's ability to handle obstacles like logs and rocks

trip meter–a device that measures how many miles you've gone on a single trip

two-stroke–an engine with in which every stroke of the piston is a power stroke

To Learn More

Freeman, Gary. *Motocross*. Radical Sports. Chicago: Heinemann Library, 2002.

Morse, Jenifer Corr. *Motorcycles*. Speed! Woodbridge, Conn.: Blackbirch Press, 2001.

Parr, Danny. *Dirt Bikes*. Wild Rides! Mankato, Minn.: Capstone Press, 2002.

Pupeza, Lori Kinstad. *Dirt Bikes*. Minneapolis: Abdo & Daughters, 1999.

Stuart, Dee. *Motorcycles*. Berkeley Heights, N.J.: Enslow Publishers, 2001.

Youngblood, Ed. *Dirt Track Racing*. Motorcycles. Mankato, Minn.: Capstone Press, 2000.

Index